ARIES

—SUN SIGN SERIES—

ALSO BY JOANNA MARTINE WOOLFOLK

Sexual Astrology

Honeymoon for Life

The Only Astrology Book You'll Ever Need

ARIES

SUN SIGN SERIES
JOANNA MARTINE WOOLFOLK

TAYLOR TRADE PUBLISHING
LANHAM • NEW YORK • BOULDER • TORONTO • PLYMOUTH, UK

Published by Taylor Trade Publishing
An imprint of The Rowman & Littlefield Publishing Group, Inc.
4501 Forbes Boulevard, Suite 200, Lanham, Maryland 20706
www.rlpgtrade.com

Estover Road, Plymouth PL6 7PY, United Kingdom

Distributed by National Book Network

British Library Cataloguing in Publication Information Available

Library of Congress Cataloging-in-Publication Data

Woolfolk, Joanna Martine.
  Aries / Joanna Martine Woolfolk.
    p. cm.—(Sun sign series)
  ISBN 978-1-58979-553-2 (pbk. : alk. paper)—ISBN 978-1-58979-528-0 (electronic)
  1. Aries (Astrology) I. Title.
  BF1727.W66 2011
  133.5'262—dc22   2011001964

∞™   The paper used in this publication meets the minimum requirements of American
National Standard for Information Sciences—Permanence of Paper for Printed Library
Materials, ANSI/NISO Z39.48-1992.

Printed in the United States of America

I dedicate this book to the memory of
William Woolfolk
whose wisdom continues to guide me,

and to
James Sgandurra
who made everything bloom again.

CONTENTS

ABOUT THE AUTHOR

Astrologer Joanna Martine Woolfolk has had a long career as an author, columnist, lecturer, and counselor. She has written the monthly horoscope for numerous magazines in the United States, Europe, and Latin America—among them *Marie Claire*, *Harper's Bazaar*, *Redbook*, *Self*, *YM*, *House Beautiful*, and *StarScroll International*. In addition to the best-selling *The Only Astrology Book You'll Ever Need*, Joanna is the author of *Sexual Astrology*, which has sold over a million copies worldwide, and *Astrology Source*, an interactive CD-ROM.

Joanna is a popular television and radio personality who has been interviewed by Barbara Walters, Regis Philbin, and Sally Jessy Raphael. She has appeared in a regular astrology segment on *New York Today* on NBC-TV and on *The Fairfield Exchange* on

CT Cable Channel 12, and she appears frequently on television and radio shows around the country. You can visit her website at www.joannamartinewoolfolk.com.

ACKNOWLEDGMENTS

Many people contribute to the creation of a book, some with ideas and editorial suggestions, and some unknowingly through their caring and love.

Among those who must know how much they helped is Jed Lyons, the elegant, erudite president of my publishers, the Rowman & Littlefield Publishing Group. Jed gave me the idea for this Sun Sign series, and I am grateful for his faith and encouragement.

Enormous gratitude also to Michael K. Dorr, my literary agent and dear friend, who has believed in me since we first met and continues to be my champion. I thank Michael for his sharp editor's eye and imbuing me with confidence.

Two people who don't know how much they give are my beloved sister and brother, Patricia G. Reynhout and Dr. John T. Galdamez. They sustain me with their unfailing devotion and support.

*We are born at a given moment, in a given place,
and like vintage years of wine, we have the
qualities of the year and of the season
in which we are born.*

CARL GUSTAV JUNG

INTRODUCTION

When my publishers suggested I write a book devoted solely to Aries, I was thrilled. I've long wanted to concentrate exclusively on your wonderful sign. You are very special in the zodiac because Aries is the first sign in the astrological lineup. You represent all that is new, fresh, and adventuresome. You always want to see what's on the other side of the mountain. You're a groundbreaker and pioneer, brave, full of conquering energy—the one who rides over obstacles because of your faith in a triumphant outcome. Especially you're known for your willingness to rush forward. Karmic teachers say you were picked to be an Aries because of your heroism and noble character in a previous life. But whether or not one believes in past lives, in *this* life you are Aries, the great leader.

These days it has become fashionable to be a bit dismissive of Sun signs (the sign that the Sun was in at the time of your birth). Some people sniff that "everyone knows about Sun signs." They say the descriptions are too "cookie-cutter," too much like cardboard figures, too inclusive (how can every Aries be the same?).

Of course every Aries is not the same! And many of these differences are not only genetic and environmental, but differences in your *charts*. Another Aries would not necessarily have your Moon sign, or Venus sign, or Ascendant. However, these are factors to consider later—after you have studied your Sun sign. (In *The Only Astrology Book You'll Ever Need*, I cover in depth differences in charts: different Planets, Houses, Ascendants, etc.)

First and foremost, you are an Aries. This is the sign the Sun was traveling through at the time of your birth.* The Sun is our most powerful planet. (In astrological terms, the Sun is referred to as a "planet" even though technically it is a "luminary.") It gives us life, warmth, energy, and food. It is the force that sustains us on Earth. The Sun is also the most important and pervasive influence in your horoscope and in many ways determines how others see you. Your Sun sign governs your individuality, your distinctive style, and your drive to fulfill your goals.

Your sign of Aries symbolizes the role you are given to play in this life. It's as if at the moment of your birth you were pushed onstage into a drama called *This Is My Life*. In this drama, you are the starring actor—and Aries is the character you play. What aspects of this character are you going to project? The Aries courage and ability to initiate? Its generosity, honesty, enthusiasm, and spirit of adventure? Or its impatience and thoughtlessness—its self-absorption and me-first pushiness? Your sign of Aries describes your journey through this life, for it is your task to evolve into a perfect Aries.

For each of us, the most interesting, most gripping subject is *self*. The longer I am an astrologer—which at this point is half my lifetime—the more I realize that what we all want to know about is ourselves. "Who am I?" you ask. You want to know what makes

---

*From our viewpoint here on Earth, the Sun travels around the Earth once each year. Within the space of that year the Sun moves through all twelve signs of the zodiac, spending approximately one month in each sign.

you tick, why you have such intense feelings, and whether others are also insecure. People ask me questions like "What kind of man should I look for?" "Why am I discontented with my job?" or "The woman I'm dating is a Gemini; will we be happy together?" They ask me if they'll ever find true love and when they will get out of a period of sadness or fear or the heavy burden of problems. They ask about their path in life and how they can find more fulfillment.

So I continue to see that the reason astrology exists is to answer questions about you. Basically, it's all about *you*. Astrology has been described as a stairway leading into your deeper self. It holds out the promise that you do not have to pass through life reacting blindly to experience, that you can, within limits, direct your own destiny and in the process reach a truer self-understanding.

Astrologically, the place to begin the study of yourself is your Sun sign. In this book, you'll read about your many positive qualities as well as your Aries issues and negative inclinations. You'll find insights into your power and potentials, advice about love and sex, career guidance, health and diet tips, and information about myriads of objects, places, concepts, and things to which Aries is attached. You'll also find topics not usually included in other astrology books—such as how Aries fits in with Chinese astrology and with numerology.

Come with me on this exploration of the "infinite variety" (in Shakespeare's phrase) of being an Aries.

Joanna Martine Woolfolk
Stamford, Connecticut
June 2011

ARIES

MARCH 21–APRIL 19

PART ONE

ALL ABOUT YOU

ILLUMINATING QUOTATIONS

"Are you able to say yes to your adventure—the adventure of the hero, the adventure of being alive?"

—Joseph Campbell, author of *The Power of Myth*, an Aries

"Acting should be bigger than life. Scripts should be bigger than life. *Life* should be bigger than life!"

—Bette Davis, actress, an Aries

"I've always had confidence. It came because I have lots of initiative. I wanted to make something of myself."

—Eddie Murphy, comedian and actor, an Aries

"You have to be really courageous about your instincts and your ideas. Otherwise, what would have been memorable will be lost."

—Francis Ford Coppola, film director and screenwriter, an Aries

YOUR ARIES PERSONALITY

YOUR MOST LIKEABLE TRAIT: Courage

The bright side of Aries: Energetic, enterprising, optimistic, open to change, idealistic

The dark side of Aries: Impulsive, opinionated, domineering, impatient, vain

Aries is energy personified—the conqueror who strives to expand its kingdom. You are passionate and courageous, impetuous and not afraid to explore the untried. The new excites you and you will always push through a barrier to find out what else there is. You're impelled to make an impact and create change, and you burn with a desire to succeed. Definitely, you're a take-charge person. You have huge vitality, a life force that can't be confined. Your Aries commanding presence exudes confidence, and you easily assume the role of leader and trailblazer. You view your life as a series of "missions"—and because you're intensely focused on attaining your goals, you're highly impatient with anyone who tries to slow you down. With your quick temper, you can be provocative and certainly aggressive.

Aries is the first sign of the zodiac, the sign that symbolizes fresh starts and new beginnings. It connotes quick changes and sudden forks in the road. Your life is marked by arriving at a certain place and then being turned in a new direction. Certainly, one can say your life is adventurous!

There is a dynamic restlessness to the Aries character. You're happiest originating new ideas and starting new plans—you're an activist and doer. If an enterprise strikes your fancy, you can't wait to plunge right in. The amusing little prayer, "Grant me patience NOW!" is typical of the Arien attitude. You're especially drawn to anything with an element of risk and the unknown. Sights your eyes have never seen before are what thrill you most. The opposite side of the scale is that you have a low threshold for boredom. Nothing drearies your spirit more than routine, and the minute you get into a rut, you frantically look for an escape hatch.

People love you because you bring excitement to their lives. You're blessed with enough energy for ten—you cheer up everyone with your childlike exuberance. When they first meet you, their instant impression is of someone exciting, vibrant, talkative. If someone brings up a topic, you will be delighted to tell in great detail exactly what you think about it. They'll be lucky if they can get a word in edgewise.

As an Aries person you gravitate toward the center of the action. You are audacious and intent on getting your own way. Since your nature is to express power, you treat opposition as an annoyance to be brushed out of the way. You are a natural leader who exudes self-confidence. From an early age you feel you're headed for success—and when your energies are ignited, you're very hard to resist.

Happily, you are also generous about helping others in a crisis. You are an openhearted friend who shares ideas and advice, and who likes to pick up the check. You have a quality of largesse. You are not interested in the small or petty. "Go for the best" is your motto.

There is nothing faint or half-hearted about an Arien. Whereas others may be more cautious, you actually enjoy living on the edge. A touch of recklessness makes you feel alive. The chase is always more thrilling than getting the goal. (As one Aries recently remarked rather insightfully, "Wanting is always better than getting.") You are willing to take a gamble, follow a dream, set your mind on a goal, and pursue it with irresistible enthusiasm. Your supreme quality of optimism attracts others. Underneath insecurity may lurk, but no one will ever know about it.

This is not to say you don't get depressed or moody. Yet the winter of despair doesn't last a week with Aries. You have an un-crackable optimism, and even in moments of self-doubt, you don't let fear sabotage you. One of the best things about being Aries is you feel that if you really want to, you can lick anything. You'll ask yourself, "What's the worst that can happen?" and having decided you can deal with it, you go ahead. People think you were born lucky, but a lot of your luck springs from your willingness to give anything a try.

It's true, though, that Aries people are notorious for taking offense at fancied slights and injuries. Hot tempers and childish tantrums abound, and your threshold of boredom is extremely low. If success is not immediate, you tend to lose interest and go in search of other excitement. As a result, patient, plodding types often get to the head of the class before you do.

Ariens have a well-deserved reputation for not finishing what they have begun. You are very short of patience, and your lack of stick-to-it-iveness is your weak spot. Also, you spend your energy in too many different ways, like the Ring Lardner hero who mounted a horse and rode off in all directions at once.

Independence is a keyword. You can turn sulky and peevish if you have to take orders. You would much rather be the world's largest lizard than the world's smallest dragon. You want to run the whole show. If you can't, you pull up stakes and look for a situation in which you can show off your style and brilliance. Should you come up against a superior force, you will bend but never break. Your aggressive and combative spirit cannot be broken by anyone—except yourself.

One of the pitfalls of being an Aries is that you're essentially self-involved. You find it hard to consider what the other person is feeling. Unless you make an effort to look outward at others and their feelings, you can easily become a spoiled brat.

Though generally sincere and honest, you will tell a white lie if it seems advantageous. You are not a very adept liar, however; others see right through you. Sometimes you lack tact and diplomacy, but no malice is intended. Sagittarians also lack this quality of tact because they don't know how to be oblique or roundabout. With you, tactlessness is an impulsive act—a careless expression of your innate force. Too often you speak without thinking and say whatever pops into your mouth, and you usually regret your impulsiveness later.

Aries is lucky with money, but has trouble holding on to it. You tend to run up big bills, live extravagantly, soar over budget. However, you usually find a way to pay off what you owe. You have too much pride to remain in anyone's debt.

In friendship, you give magnanimously if someone is in need, but you want to get credit for your good deeds. In the garden of Aries, there are few shrinking violets.

You are creative, openhearted, high-spirited, pioneering, and also vain, feisty, and impatient. Those who deal with you on an intimate basis will have one chief problem: how are they going to keep up the pace?

THE INNER YOU

You like to be in charge—you want to control your own projects and plans and not be under anyone else's thumb. You have an intense drive to succeed and put a lot of pressure on yourself. Inside, you're filled with nervous energy and worry about how you're going to handle everything. At times you suffer from insomnia. You hate to be bored; you're always looking for something different—new people and places that promise excitement and adventure. You have very little patience; you need to practice sticking things out. You're also impatient with people who can't resolve a problem. You believe in taking action. What you do have are great generosity and enthusiasm. And although you suffer from occasional self-doubt, you know that if you really want to do something, you can!

HOW OTHERS SEE YOU

Your upbeat, magnetic personality pulls people toward you—you bring excitement into their lives. They envy your aggressiveness in meeting a challenge. Whatever the problem, you give the impression that you have an answer ready. You're also admired for your honesty; you don't gloss over difficulties. What people don't like is your tendency toward bossiness and your deserved reputation for being sharp-tongued. They're afraid to cross you in an argument because they know you can cut them to the quick.

GUARD AGAINST: Becoming an Obsessive, Take-Charge Tyrant

You were born impatient; you want everything right away. You rush into a project shooing away what impedes, issuing orders, bossing people around. Being so focused and with a great propensity toward thoughtlessness, you don't see what others are feeling or that you're trampling on their feet. Everything you say and do is filtered through the prism of *me, myself, and I*—and you can be extremely shortsighted and short-tempered. You erupt when people can't read your mind and grant your wishes. You have a dominant personality to begin with and, unchecked, your Aries force-of-will becomes a heat-seeking missile out to get its target.

You're definitely self-centered, but this does have its positive side. To have a healthy sense of self is a wonderful gift, and certainly your strength lies in your assertiveness. You're direct and dynamic, filled with inexhaustible optimism and a great deal of boldness. Your hair-trigger brain snatches up a plan of action, and no one can get as much done as you in so short a time. Astrology teaches that the psychological motivation of Aries is to assert your will.

However, like any power (electric, steam, nuclear), your domineering Aries force must be harnessed. Otherwise it will run roughshod over your whole personality and damage you and others. You need to guard against becoming brutal.

You have so much to counteract your Aries arrogance, for at your core you're also extraordinarily generous. You want to pour out to others your gifts of love, aliveness, passion, and *joie de vivre*. You give your time, energy, and financial help. Most of all, because of your great sense of possibility, you give others courage. Allow your astonishing Aries luminosity to balance your need to feed your ego.

YOUR GREATEST CHALLENGE: Learning Moderation

This does not mean quieting down, sublimating your energy, slinking away, or lessening the excitement you generate. You're a mover and shaker who will always strive to make the most of every moment. You're on a feverish quest to bring a concept into being (your creative drive) and enlarge your life. You're a superstar and, in whatever you do, you need to be in the forefront. It's as if at the moment of your birth a path is already cut—and it's straight up to the top. For you not to give full vent to your jet-propulsion is like being caged. You grow dull, detached, and droopy, and your impatient quality turns into anxiety and worry that can tear down what you're trying to build.

Moderation—meaning not excessive or extreme—is your key. By pacing yourself, you won't burn out quickly and leave projects unfinished. By keeping your impulsiveness in check, you won't make faulty decisions. By not speaking before you think, you'll develop tact and people charm. You need to shut the door on your hyperactivity, and look at your gargantuan goals in small sections—one step at a time, one objective every day. Aries's lessons are balance, moderation, learning to behave more like the turtle than the hare so that you can go the distance.

YOUR ALTER EGO

Astrology gives us many tools in our lives to help manage our struggles and solve problems. One of these tools is to reach into your opposite sign in the zodiac—your polarity. For you, Aries, this is Libra, sign of partnership and relationships. Libra is known for being the peaceable diplomat and blending seamlessly into partnership and alliances. Charm, sweetness, and geniality are their stock in trade. Librans have esthetic taste, decorum, good manners, and social grace. They instinctively sense what is appropriate in every situation.

Libra is gifted with the ability to "see"—to see how to make a setting beautiful, to see how others are feeling. They're supersensitive to the reactions of those around them and whether tension may be brewing. Tactful and tolerant, Libra strives to please and placate and keep harmony. Basically, Libra is a balancing force—its own life's journey is to find balance between self and others.

Like you, Libra is intelligent and communicative. Aries and Libra are both Cardinal signs and share a love of new adventure and a forward-looking attitude. You're both highly pleasure-oriented, fond of a well-appointed lifestyle, and you're both creative. But unlike you, Libra makes room for the other. Indeed, Libra's focus is to be in a relationship. It wants to meet the other halfway, get feedback, and be part of a union—whether this is a career alliance or a romantic bond. Libra doesn't view others as adversaries and obstacles in the way.

You, Aries, are highly competitive. The point is to prevail, to gain victory. But the price is high, for in many ways you're always looking over your shoulder to see who is gaining on you.

In times of stressful conflict with others, you can tap into Libran qualities of appeasement and conciliation. This certainly doesn't mean being run over roughshod and giving up. It means recognizing that you do yourself most good by coming to the table to talk things over—that with cooperation and compromise, you win over people and gain allies. If you can blend Libra's diplomacy and art of collaboration with your Aries courage and driving force, you have an unbeatable combination. By looking at a situation from the point of view of the *other*, you will cement the deal, strengthen the relationship, get your goal every time.

By the same token, Libra has a great deal it can take from Aries. Primary is your sense of *self*. Without this, Libra is doomed to live in the shadows, depending on others for validation. Libra needs to learn from you how to tap into its own sense of confidence and wholeness. The Aries essence is to believe in yourself—whereas Libra gives power to the other. Instead of making the priority being approved of and liked, Libra should look to you to discover how to be a hero to itself. Indeed, this is a lesson we all can learn from you, Aries!

ARIES IN LOVE

It's superfluous to say you have fiery emotions because you have practically no other kind. You're the seeker of passion—high voltage surrounds you—and you want to experience the whole gamut of erotic fervor. You're a fully stocked fireplace, with logs, kindling, and paper, and all you need is the touch of a match to set you on fire.

Yet unlike, say, a sensuous and sentimental Cancer, or a sexually dominant Scorpio, you're an *adventurer* when it comes to love and sex. You project an air of daring. Without words, you signal to potential lovers that you're willing to try anything, cross boundaries, take risks emotionally. You're impetuous; you leap before you look. You're a wild romantic who's far more attracted to the glamorous razzle-dazzle and fantasy than you are to a real flesh-and-blood person. Indeed, you can be a fool for love if it comes at you like a larger-than-life movie.

When you're first attracted to someone you whirl into action, and it becomes a fascinating game of seeing how fast you can capture that person. Your ruling planet is Mars, ancient god of fire and war, and you were born with a warrior spirit. The hunt, the chase, is irresistible, and an exhilarating pursuit only fuels your quick-tinder passions. On some level (even unconsciously), your goal is to make the other person your love slave.

Sexually, you tend to be the one who calls the signals and controls the action. You're intent on your own pleasure, and you like erotic positions that make your lover crave you more. Every sex encounter (even with the same lover) takes on the drama of a conquest. In the throes of sexual emotion you don't know the meaning of restraint.

A love affair with you is not easy. You're high maintenance. You want freedom and total togetherness and ecstasy all at once. You want to be swept away by a bold lover who doesn't have too many interests other than you. Definitely, your chemistry works best with someone who tries to dominate you—even if you're a male Aries who claims to dislike domineering women. With a lover who can create an aura of competitiveness (subtle, playful, or otherwise), you two merge into a combustible rivalry/friendship that keeps you slightly on edge. You can easily become bored, but a spirited partner you can't take entirely for granted continues to fan your interest. A bit of unsureness in the relationship—a lover who tweaks at your jealousy once in a while—keeps you on your toes.

Psychologically, you're uncomfortable with weakness (in yourself and in others). Therefore, you have a tendency to repress your own frailties and then blame your lover for not being strong enough. In love, you need to learn to live and let live. Notice that your take-charge relationship style is often a cover-up for your vulnerability and a way of not letting the other merge into your deeper emotional core.

However, you do adore attention, and with your charm and magnetism you'll always attract admirers. Adulation feeds and fills you. Actually, the way to your heart is through your ego. And much as your eye may wander, when you fall in love for real you do so with all your heart. You have the emotional power to make your lover feel as if he or she has never been loved as ravishingly. You also have an enormous capacity for loyalty. You become your lover's staunchest ally who'll fight side by side with him or her. You give all of yourself—all your verve and dynamism and energy—to creating a grand passion. In turn, what you need most is to be understood and appreciated for your magnificent qualities and to feel your lover is totally devoted to you.

TIPS FOR THOSE WHO WANT TO ATTRACT ARIES

Don't be timid. Faint heart never won Aries, male or female. Let Aries people know how much you admire them right at the beginning. Aries people will never think you brash if you are paying them a compliment. They feel they deserve it. Be a bit careful, though, about laying it on too thick. They adore being showered with flattery, but they do have a way of spotting insincerity.

Aries people think of themselves as intellectuals, so don't appeal to them purely on a physical plane. They will enjoy a lively discussion of theater, music, politics, or even more esoteric subjects such as history, art, or philosophy.

A good suggestion for a date early in the relationship is a sporting event. (With Aries, it can never be more than a suggestion.) They are enthusiastic sports fans. If you don't know much about the game you're watching, let the Arien explain it to you. Aries will do so in a way that will make it interesting and exciting.

Before an important date, take a nice long nap. Aries is no clock-watcher, and the fun may go on and on into the wee hours.

Aries people pick up steam while everyone else is running out of gas.

By all means, bring your problems to Aries. There is nothing they like better than to be asked for advice. They are generous with their time, counsel, money, and sympathy. And there's an additional advantage: No Aries is in doubt as to what should be done in any given situation. You'll get a forthright, black-and-white, no-quibbles-or-evasions answer.

Important: Never try to dictate to an Aries. They don't know how to take orders. If you want to put an idea into his or her head, do it so that Aries thinks the idea originated there.

ARIES'S EROGENOUS ZONES: Tips for Those with an Aries Lover

Our bodies are very sensitive to the touch of another human being. The special language of touching is understood on a level more basic than speech. Each sign is linked to certain zones and areas of the body that are especially receptive and can receive sexual messages through touch. Many books and manuals have been written about lovemaking, but few pay attention to the unique knowledge of erogenous zones supplied by astrology. You can use astrology to become a better, more sensitive lover.

For Aries people, the nerve endings in the face and head are especially sensitive. Gentle stroking of the hair and scalp is something they respond to favorably.

Aries woman loves to have her hair combed and played with. If you nibble Aries man's ear, you will send him a definite sexual message. Other stimulations that people of this sign respond to are feather-light strokes of the lips with your fingertips, and gentle kisses on their closed eyelids.

One technique that will relax Aries and put her or him in the mood for love is to travel a path with your fingertips from the base of the hairline at the back of the neck up to the top of the skull. Your fingers should move in small circles that vibrate the scalp. Use a light but firm pressure. Repeat this pathway from neck to top of the crown until the entire head has been massaged. This technique is also extremely useful for relieving headaches due to nervous tension, to which Aries is subject.

ARIES'S AMOROUS COMBINATIONS: YOUR LOVE PARTNERS

ARIES AND ARIES

This can be a passionate affair. You are Fire signs who meet and mate in a blaze of sexual fervor, but neither of you is content with an inferior role. The Aries female tends to dominate (generally because domineering females have to try harder to get their way than domineering males). However, there will be fierce competition to be number one, which makes for a relationship in which the jabs and digs keep flying. Eventually, the flare-ups and heavy cannonading take their toll in the bedroom, and what starts out so promisingly ends in disharmony. The prognosis is a little better if each of you has outside interests and/or a career separate from the other. When your energies are diverted into other areas, conflict between you two becomes a bit more playful and less destructive.

ARIES AND TAURUS

Aries and Taurus are both highly sensual signs, but Aries may be annoyed by the deliberate pace and unimaginative lovemaking of Taurus. Taurus is a homebody, while you definitely are not. Aries is a restless seeker looking for new experiences. Once Taurus has found its comfortable niche, he or she wants to stay in it, cozy and secure. Aries is open to the new and needs a great deal of attention from the world. Taurus is possessive and jealous, is set in its ways, and views your need to be an individual as a personal rejection. Taurus is good at making money, but you're even better at spending it. With so little in common, the long haul can be hard going. Still, if you two hang on long enough, Aries will come to appreciate Taurus's steadiness and dependability.

ARIES AND GEMINI

You won't bore each other because you both love to talk. (It's a close contest, but Gemini will probably win.) And you share a special compatibility, for Gemini is as restless and eager to try new things as you are. There are no inhibitions on either side. Gemini is clever enough to counter your need to dominate. Gemini may seek extra outside stimulation, but is discreet about it. Your minds mesh well—as an Aries, you're dynamic and intelligent, and Gemini is versatile and ingenious. Though both signs tend to have poor staying power, your emotional energies blend into a sparkly, sexy friendship that can last. Aries is likely to be the leader sexually, and Gemini delights in thinking up variations to keep your interest at a peak. The signals are definitely go.

ARIES AND CANCER

At the beginning you're fascinated with each other, but sexual attraction fades in the face of many temperamental differences. Aries leaps into love without looking, whereas cautious Cancer moves into a relationship slowly. Cancer loves hearth and home; you hate being tied down. Resentments build up, and you argue over trifles. Your Aries sharp tongue wounds vulnerable Cancer. Cancer broods over hurt feelings and asserts itself only indirectly—which irritates confrontational you. Aries enjoys a good fight, whereas Cancer expresses its anger by withdrawing. The more aggressive you are, the more defensive Cancer becomes. There's too little compatibility to work with. When Cancer starts to nag, you look for the way out.

ARIES AND LEO

Both of you have egos to burn and both like to lead. Aggressive Aries wouldn't dream of taking second place, and kingly Leo needs constant admiration. Usually you two can work it out by having Leo play the emperor and Aries play the general. The trick is for neither to take the other all that seriously. It's a fine, combustible sexual match, for you're both fiery and romantic. Both go in for extravagant gestures—flowers, champagne, first-class dining— and erotic lovemaking. In addition, your Aries attitude toward life is optimistic and enthusiastic, and Leo has an expansive outlook. You're sparked by Leo's dash and brio. If neither tries to deflate the other—and if you two can find room to compromise about who dominates whom—this should be a happy mating.

ARIES AND VIRGO

Aries's boldness intrigues shy, reserved Virgo for a time. But you two have totally different ideas about what should happen in the bedroom—and elsewhere. Aries's passions are impulsive and direct. Virgo's sexuality is more enigmatic and takes time to be revealed. In other areas, Aries is full of exciting new plans and ideas, and insists on being boss. Virgo is critical and fussy, and likes things to be done the way Virgo wants. An essential difference in your temperaments is that Virgo wants to improve the way the world is run—and Aries wants to *change* it. You're drawn to risk, the untried, and the grand adventure. Virgo disapproves of your extravagance; you think Virgo cold and carping. You two end up making war, not love.

ARIES AND LIBRA

Aries and Libra are opposite signs in the zodiac, and immediately a powerful attraction ignites between you. In certain areas, each supplies what the other lacks. For one, your Aries aggressiveness arouses Libra's sensual potential. Your love life together may be unconventional and deeply erotic. However, Libra really wants peace, quiet, and harmony, while you want action and adventure. Both like social life, entertaining, and pleasure, but both are restless in different ways. In time Libra will look for someone less demanding, and Aries will find someone more adoring. Marvelous affair; poor marriage. Yet if each of you could see that each is deficient in what the other has—and eventually adopt the good qualities of the other—this team has the potential of becoming a tightly knit, long-term partnership.

ARIES AND SCORPIO

Love can be a bonfire between you two. Both Aries and Scorpio are physical, energetic, and passionate, and your lovemaking is rapturous. Sexually, everything should be fine—it's the emotional side of the relationship neither can handle. Each has a forceful personality and wants to control the other. Manipulative Scorpio has a penchant for making life complicated, whereas Aries likes it simple—great adventure, grand passion, and the freedom to live on a larger scale than others do. In the end, Scorpio's jealousy may prove the undoing. Your many outside interests make Scorpio feel insecure, and this brings out Scorpio's tyrannical streak. Aries won't take orders, and Scorpio will never take a backseat. An unstable partnership with a low ignition point.

ARIES AND SAGITTARIUS

Sagittarius is a perfect temperamental match for Aries. You're both active, spontaneous people who like socializing, have extravagant tastes in common, and enjoy the good life. Both look outward for stimulation—you two like to travel, explore, and head out for the undiscovered. Your lifestyles integrate well because you're free spirits who embrace the next new adventure—though there may be some conflict because both tend to be impulsive and brutally frank. Arguments can reach the boiling point. Aries's forceful sexual approach is not always playful Sagittarius's style. Aries wants adoration, and Sagittarius tends to be detached. However, you both have wonderful senses of humor and enjoy each other's company. If you make it in the bedroom, you'll make it everywhere else.

ARIES AND CAPRICORN

Your Aries taste for innovation and experimentation may not please conservative Capricorn. Aries is restless, fiery, impulsive; Capricorn is ordered, settled, practical. Capricorn needs to dominate, and so does Aries. Problems also crop up over money—Aries is extravagant, Capricorn is security-minded. Though you're both goal oriented, Capricorn's aim is to be a powerful achiever, whereas trailblazing Aries wants the adulation of others. Aries has a buoyant outlook; Capricorn is terribly serious. Oddly enough, the auguries are better for the long haul than the short. You have sensual intensity in common, and Aries's responsive sexual nature meets its match in Capricorn's deep-seated passions. And Capricorn's strength and endurance will in time win your respect.

ARIES AND AQUARIUS

You're well suited temperamentally—both are active and ambitious, enjoy a wide range of interests, and love to communicate. You're immediately attracted to each other's minds. You are also equally eager for sexual adventure. Depending on whim, Aquarius may or may not let Aries take the lead. Both are independent—Aquarius even more than Aries—and Aries may at times feel neglected. You are more comfortable with intimacy than Aquarius. Aquarius's affections are for ideas and distant goals, whereas you're a romantic who focuses on your lover. You find the Aquarian unpredictability exciting, but you also never feel entirely secure. However, with a bit of tact and understanding on both sides, this is a great affair that could turn into something even better.

ARIES AND PISCES

Aries will draw Pisces out of that self-protective shell, and in turn you'll be hypnotized by Pisces's seductive and mysterious sexuality. Pisces has erotic desires and secret longings, and Aries is just the one to help Pisces act them out. The boldness and confidence of Aries plus Pisces's intuitions and fantasies add up to an eventful union. Personality differences complement each other. Aries is self-assured and vivacious—Pisces is somewhat shy and easily led. Aries likes to be dominant; Pisces likes having someone to lean on. It's true that Pisces's supersensitive feelings can sometimes be ridden over roughshod by you, who tend to barrel through life not noticing the nuances. But for a happy coupling, this requires just a little more tact on your part.

YOUR ARIES CAREER PATH

You're the one who rides in and injects new hope into every situation. You are known for being a charismatic leader—your secret is you ignite enthusiasm in others. This potent chemistry with people, plus the fact you're brash and ambitious, allows you to rise quickly in your career. Your stimulating style makes an immediate impact and, since you're never happy sitting on the sidelines, you speak up, set things into motion, and go for every opportunity.

A reason you're formidable in your work is you have rock bottom confidence in yourself. This isn't to say you never feel insecure or anxious. But somehow you're able to make these feelings fuel you, not foil you. You're not afraid to give something a try. You don't hem and haw, worrying about making a mistake. To you, any action is better than none, so you impatiently brush aside negative thinking and pursue risks. You believe in making your own luck. As an Aries, you're all about becoming the generating force in your life (not allowing outside forces to control you). Yes, you've had your share of false starts and wrong decisions, but you're courageous about following your instincts.

Interestingly, success to you is not necessarily measured by monetary gain. You're highly creative and often gauge your success in terms of accolades. You need applause. Your energy comes from the feeling of being *connected*.

The best professions for you are those in which you're in charge and can work independently or break new ground. Many Aries people form their own company. You can be an extraordinary entrepreneur. You're a fast thinker and have a gift for words, so you do well in writing, journalism, advertising, and public relations. Because you're highly imaginative and expressive, the performing arts call to you—you're drawn to the "stage," whether this arena is acting or public speaking. Your Aries assurance and attractiveness are great assets for film and television careers, as well as sales and marketing.

It's true that as an assertive Fire sign, you have the reputation of being selfish and self-seeking. Yes, Aries is the sign of being out in front (you're the first sign of the zodiac), and you're in a hurry to get to the top. But in general your selfishness stems more from thoughtlessness than avarice. You pursue what you want with immense vigor, and don't stop to think that what you're doing might overwhelm or damage others. You're hell-bent on taking *your* action and it doesn't occur to you until too late that this may destroy a business relationship or turn someone against you. You're the kind who doesn't like taking orders, even suggestions, and your first answer to others' ideas is usually "No." These Aries inclinations of impatience, insensitivity, and self-importance work against you in career alliances. You would have greater success dealing with people if you'd stop to think and not say the first thing that flies into your head.

Still, you have so much in your character that can lead you to your aspirations. By being a pioneer and going your own way, you find surprising opportunities. In spite of chaotic conditions, you have laser vision to see clearly to your goal. Your supercharged daring meets problems head-on. And your ability to not get discouraged is legendary. You burn with a hunger for life, and your destiny is to do heroic deeds.

ARIES AND HEALTH:
ADVICE FROM ASTROLOGY

For optimum well-being, Aries needs exercise. You have an abundance of energy that, unused, will become blocked and make you depressed. Inactivity slows down your thinking and makes you feel your life is out of balance. You're like a racehorse that needs to stay in prime running condition. Exercise will keep your body toned, your mind alert, and your spirits joyful. Aries rules the head, and you're prone to ailments such as headaches and eyestrain. You can cope by being vigilant about what triggers your disorders. Often, too, your head swirls with a clutter of confused thoughts. Slow down so that you don't suffer physical and mental exhaustion. Aries tends to be accident prone—be aware of mishaps waiting to happen and take precautions (e.g., use a pot holder, wear a helmet). In general, Aries is exceedingly strong in health and vitality.

Advice and useful tips about health are among the most important kinds of information that astrology provides. Health and well-being are of paramount concern to human beings. Love, money, or career takes second place, for without good health we cannot enjoy anything in life.

Astrology and medicine have had a long marriage. Hippocrates (born around 460 B.C.), the Greek philosopher and physician who is considered the father of medicine, said, "A physician without a knowledge of astrology has no right to call himself a physician." Indeed, up until the eighteenth century, the study of astrology and its relationship to the body was very much a part of a doctor's training. When a patient became ill, a chart was immediately drawn up. This guided the doctor in both diagnosis and treatment, for the chart would tell when the crisis would come and what medicine would help. Of course, modern Western doctors no longer use astrology to treat illness. However, astrology can still be a useful tool in helping to understand and maintain our physical well-being.

THE PART OF THE BODY RULED BY ARIES

Each sign of the zodiac rules or governs a specific part of the body. These associations date back to the beginning of astrology. Curiously, the part of the body that a sign rules is in some ways the strongest and in other ways the weakest area for natives of that sign.

Your sign of Aries rules the head and face. Others can often spot the fact that you're an Aries because of your fine facial bone structure and a shining, healthy head of hair. Sometimes Aries people have a birthmark or mole on the face. The head is associated with thinking and perception, and you tend to be a sharp, shrewd thinker who uses common sense.

But you are also subject to headaches, including migraines, head congestion, and sinus conditions. You're prone to minor injuries around the head and face, and should use protective headgear if taking part in strenuous sports. You have a tendency to overwork yourself and overtax your energy. You're prey to eyestrain and to having problems with your teeth.

When excited or frustrated, you'll often get red in the face. If you have a fever, it tends to reach a high degree in a short period of time. However, you have strong recuperative powers and can fight off illness very rapidly.

In addition to each sign governing a specific area of the body, the ruling *planets* of the signs are associated with various glands in the body. Your glands release hormones that keep your body functioning. Aries's ruling planet, Mars, is linked to the adrenal glands. These are the glands that pump adrenaline into the bloodstream during times of stress and emergency. You are known for your impetuosity and excitability, qualities associated with your dynamic planet Mars. Mars also rules the muscular system and the sex glands. You are active, have excellent muscle coordination, and are noted for your energetic sexuality.

DIET AND HEALTH TIPS FOR ARIES

Because you're usually busy, active, and on the go, you need a well-balanced diet to maintain good health and energy. Aries's cell salt* is potassium phosphate. This mineral builds brain cells and replenishes the liver. As an Aries, you expend so much energy that often your supply of this mineral is depleted and must be replenished. Lack of potassium phosphate can cause depression.

---

*Cell salts (also known as *tissue salts*) are mineral compounds found in human tissue cells. These minerals are the only substances our cells cannot produce by themselves. The life of cells is relatively short, and the creation of new cells depends on the presence of these minerals.

Foods rich in this mineral and therefore beneficial to include in your diet are tomatoes, beans (red kidney, navy, lima), brown rice, lentils, walnuts, olives, onions, lettuce, cauliflower, cucumber, spinach, broccoli, brussels sprouts, veal, swordfish, flounder, figs, bananas, dried uncooked apricots, and pumpkin. A healthy diet should also include milk, which is good for teeth and bones.

Salt and liquor are two enemies that Aries in particular should avoid. Too much salt affects bones and arteries; liquor overstimulates and reacts negatively on the kidneys. Enjoy your meals in a quiet, serene atmosphere—avoid eating too quickly or under stressful conditions. You should drink plenty of water and get adequate rest and relaxation.

With Aries ruling the head and face, one of your most striking assets is your winning smile—and your smile depends on simple dental-care habits. Brush your teeth thoroughly twice a day, and floss once a day. Replace your toothbrush often. Visit your dentist twice a year for regular checkups and cleanings. It's tempting to be lazy about your teeth, but remember that an investment of ten minutes a day is a lot less expensive (not to mention less painful) than periodontal surgery.

THE DECANATES AND CUSPS OF ARIES

Decanate and *cusp* are astrological terms that subdivide your Sun sign. These subdivisions further define and emphasize certain qualities and character traits of your Sun sign, Aries.

WHAT IS A DECANATE?

Each astrological sign is divided into three parts, and each part is called a *decanate* or a *decan* (the terms are used interchangeably).

The word comes from the Greek word *dekanoi*, meaning "ten days apart." The Greeks took their word from the Egyptians, who divided their year into 360 days.* The Egyptian year had twelve months of thirty days each, and each month was further divided into three sections of ten days each. It was these ten-day sections that the Greeks called *dekanoi*.

Astrology still divides the zodiac into decanates. There are twelve signs in the zodiac, and each sign is divided into three decanates. You might picture each decanate as a room. You were born

---

*The Egyptians soon found out that a 360-day year was inaccurate, and so added on five extra days. These were feast days and holidays, and not counted as real days.

in the sign of Aries, which consists of three rooms (decanates). In which room of Aries were you born?

The zodiac is a 360-degree circle. Each decanate is ten degrees of that circle, or about ten days long, since the Sun moves through the zodiac at approximately the rate of one degree per day. (This is not exact, because not all of our months contain thirty days.)

The decanate of a sign does not change the basic characteristics of that sign, but it does refine and individualize the sign's general characteristics. If you were born, say, in the second decanate of Aries, it does not change the fact you are Aries. It does indicate that you have somewhat special characteristics, different from those of Aries people born in the first decanate or the third decanate.

Finally, each decanate has a specific planetary ruler, sometimes called a subruler because it does not usurp the overall rulership of your sign. The subruler can only enhance and add to the distinct characteristics of your decanate. For example, your entire sign of Aries is ruled by Mars, but the second decanate of Aries is subruled by the Sun. The influence of the Sun, the subruler, combines with the overall authority of Mars to make the second decanate of Aries unlike any other in the zodiac.

FIRST DECANATE OF ARIES

March 21 through March 31
Keyword: Inspiration
Constellation: Andromeda, the Chained Woman. She was freed of her chains by Perseus, the Rescuer. This constellation symbolizes the power of love.
Planetary subruler: Mars

Mars is both your ruler and subruler, giving your personality extra force and impact. You are a dominant person and can sometimes be too aggressive. In an argument or clash of wills, you ride right over the opposition. You are impetuous and energetic, and tend to throw yourself into activities with all your heart. A person of conviction, you will never take an action that you think is wrong. Indeed, your code of honor sets you apart and gives you nobility. You are a clear, incisive thinker and can carry a plan to conclusion. What makes you shine is your ability to say *yes*—it's the secret to your success. Among your nicest qualities is your gift for inspiring confidence in others. At times you tire yourself out because you don't know when to stop. You also tend to monopolize conversations.

SECOND DECANATE OF ARIES

April 1 through April 10

Keyword: Innovation

Constellation: Cetus, the Whale or Sea Monster, tied to two fishes and led by a lamb. Cetus symbolizes energy harnessed to imagination and love.

Planetary subruler: The Sun

The Sun in this decanate adds to the power of Aries's Mars, which gives your character dignity, pride, and vitality. You have an ardent and excitable love nature, and your sexual energy is high. You adore romantic attention—you even have a touch of gullibility that at times can lead you down the wrong emotional path. The Sun here indicates a great fondness for change. You are never content to take things as they come. Because you are ambitious, you go out and try to put your mark on the world. Others tend to cluster around you, for you have *joie de vivre* and a magnetic personality. More than the other two decanates of Aries, you seek pleasure out of life. You have a taste for the expensive and can be quite imperious if you don't get what you want. A liking for too much good food is one of your downfalls.

THIRD DECANATE OF ARIES

April 11 through April 19
Keyword: Foresight
Constellation: Cassiopeia, a beautiful queen seated on her throne who symbolizes good judgment. Down through the ages she has been a celestial guide to travelers.
Planetary subruler: Jupiter

The expansive qualities of Jupiter combine with Aries's Mars to give you a wide and lofty outlook, and a love of ambitious ideas and travel. You resent restriction of any kind and prize your personal freedom. For you, the perfect life is to be successful doing something creative, where you are in charge and call all the shots. Your sense of adventure often takes you far from home. You like to find out new information, to explore different fields of knowledge. The occult interests you. You are shrewd and clever in business matters, and may possess an insight or sixth sense about other people. There is a warmhearted geniality about you that allows you to make friends easily. At times you can be too extravagant with money. In love, you believe magic can happen. Early in your life, your search for passion can lead you to many lovers.

WHAT IS A CUSP?

A *cusp* is the point at which a new astrological sign begins.* Thus, the cusp of Aries means the point at which Aries begins. (The word comes from the Latin word *cuspis*, meaning "point.")

When someone speaks of being "born on the cusp," that person is referring to a birth time at or near the beginning or the end of an astrological sign. For example, if you were born on April 19, you were born on the cusp of Taurus, the sign that begins on April 20. Indeed, depending on what year you were born, your birth time might even be in the first degree of Taurus. People born on the very day a sign begins or ends are often confused about what sign they really are—a confusion made more complicated by the fact that the Sun does not move into or out of a sign at *exactly* the same moment (or even day) each year. There are slight time differences from year to year. Therefore, if you are an Aries born on March 21 or April 19, you'll find great clarity consulting a computer chart that tells you exactly where the Sun was at the very moment you were born.

As for what span of time constitutes being born on the cusp, the astrological community holds various opinions. Some astrologers claim *cusp* means being born only within the first two days or last two days of a sign (though many say this is too narrow a time frame). Others say it can be as much as within the first ten days or last ten days of a sign (which many say is too wide an interpretation). The consensus is that you were born on the cusp if your birthday is within the first *five* days or last *five* days of a sign.

*In a birth chart, a cusp is also the point at which an astrological House begins.

The question hanging over cusp-born people is, "What sign am I really?" They feel they straddle the border of two different countries. To some extent, this is true. If you were born on the cusp, you're under the influence of both signs. However, much like being a traveler leaving one country and crossing into another, you must actually *be* in one country—you can't be in two countries at the same time. One sign is always a stronger influence, and that sign is almost invariably the sign that the Sun was actually in (in other words, your Sun sign). The reason I say "almost" is that in rare cases a chart may be so heavily weighted with planets in a certain sign that the person more keenly feels the influence of that specific sign.

For example, I have a client who was born in the evening on April 19. On that evening, the Sun was leaving Aries and entering Taurus. At the moment of her birth the Sun was still in Aries, so technically speaking she is an Aries. However, the Sun was only a couple hours away from being in Taurus, and this person has the Moon, Mercury, and Saturn all in Taurus. She has always felt like a Taurus and always behaved as a Taurus.

This, obviously, is an unusual case. Generally, the Sun is the most powerful planetary influence in a chart. Even if you were born with the Sun on the very tip of the first or last degree of Aries, Aries is your Sun sign—and this is the sign you will most feel like.

Still, the influence of the approaching sign or of the sign just ending is present, and you will probably sense that mixture in yourself.

BORN MARCH 21 THROUGH MARCH 25

You are Aries with Pisces tendencies. You are headstrong and impulsive, but part of you longs for peace and solitude. You resent it when others intrude on or interfere with your plans. You like to pursue your own thing (often something creative), and not necessarily for an audience—though you do love positive feedback. You were born with an intuitive sense that makes you a wise counselor; you have empathy for those in need. You're apt to have more sensitivity (and perhaps a tiny bit less self-confidence) than the sign of Aries is generally known for. Your intellectual powers are especially keen, and you enjoy probing into new areas and coming up with different ideas. You are clearly an individual. Warmth and sympathy come easily to you. Generally, you are fond of entertaining and get along well with people. Your lovemaking tends to be passionate, and acting out fantasy is very much part of your erotic technique.

BORN APRIL 15 THROUGH APRIL 19

You are Aries with Taurus tendencies. You are impatient, high-strung, and volatile, but also determined and at times very stubborn. Ariens have the reputation for not finishing what they begin, but you are able to see a project through to the end. You like to be the one in charge, and your reaction to disorder and sloppiness is irritation. You're an excellent provider for those you love and can take on huge responsibility without a second's misgiving. Powerful creativity runs through your veins. Your taste is original and unusual, and with your artistic eye you have a talent for making money. You have the magic combination of being able to see the creative picture and also manage the business side of a project. Emotions are a dominant factor in your life. People always know they can get an honest reaction from you. You are fiery and romantic and intensely sexual. You have strong feelings, whether it be anger or joy or love.

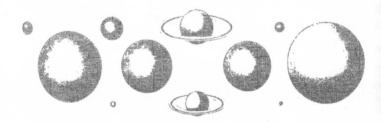

YOUR SPECIAL DAY OF BIRTH

MARCH 21

You're impetuous and impatient, but so loving others forgive your snappish ways. Literally, your arms stretch out to others. You're abundantly generous, don't engage in pretense, and haven't a malicious bone in your body.

MARCH 22

You have intense focus—you drive hard toward your goals and are your own worst critic. But when you're in relax-mode, you're a softie. Love brings out your protectiveness.

MARCH 23

People are struck by your probing mind. The fact that you're constantly pondering adds to your general mercurial quality. Emotionally, you're complicated—the key is you need to be needed.

MARCH 24

You have high style and are a great enjoyer, but secretly you crave a simple life. Love will certainly never be simple, but it can be grand if you listen to your inner instincts.

MARCH 25

You have "energizer" dynamism that seizes attention. You're in the forefront of your profession. Love follows an uneven path, but once the heartache and questionable choices are over, you happily settle down.

MARCH 26

You cut through others' fuzzy thinking and denial, and zero in on what's real. You're brilliant in business and even more so in emotional matters. You're an extraordinarily passionate lover.

MARCH 27

You have star quality, not the least because you give of yourself to others. You're a genuine diamond! Creatively, you need space of your own, and in love need a partner who has your intuitive insights.

MARCH 28

You're described as steady, yet beneath your cool demeanor you struggle to keep your "crazy psyche" under control. You're a dreamer, a doer, a warrior, and a lover.

MARCH 29

You're careful in your thinking, which creates a semblance of order in your life. Basically, you have superpowerful emotions, and when you invest them in a project or person the results are volcanic.

MARCH 30

You have an independent streak—your drive is to carve out a creation of your own. Learn to channel your versatile talents. Romantically, you're a charmer with a roving eye who is also deeply loyal.

MARCH 31

You have a strong inner core. Though your life is like a startling soap opera, you're sturdy because you know who you are. What makes you special is your to-the-end-of-the-line commitment to those you love.

APRIL 1

You're certainly not the "April Fool." From the time you were a child you assumed responsibility, and your mental brilliance awes others. But in contrast to your cool brain, in love you're a wild romantic.

APRIL 2

You're both a ram and a lamb. You have tender kindness for others and, at the same time, are a self-starter and fierce go-getter. In love, you're an idealist; over time you become wiser in your choices.

APRIL 3

You're never content to stand on the sidelines. You're openhearted, giving, and very involved. You were born with a quest—to learn, discover, and explore. Emotionally you're restless, though capable of deep love.

APRIL 4

You have imaginative far vision, but need to learn to take credit for your ideas. You find fulfillment in creating on your own. Emotionally, you search for stability although your love life is often chaotic.

APRIL 5

Laughter and new opportunity are your watchwords. You're no stranger to the dark corners of life, but you concentrate on the positive. You have innate charisma—romantic partners are drawn to your special sexual allure.

APRIL 6

You're a fixed point in a world that turns—a strong center for others. Yet you're also filled with childlike enthusiasm for new adventure. Love sometimes confuses you because your heart is so trusting.

APRIL 7

You burn with intensity—creatively, emotionally, and in your intellectual pursuits. Lovers find you a handful, though you'd say you're a pussycat. Basically, you need passion in love and work, and then you're content.

APRIL 8

You're supertalented (full of creativity), warm, and sensitive, and you have an elfin quality. Your mind is mischievous and fun-loving, as well as probing. You're very romantic and need deep intimacy.

APRIL 9

People respond to your expansive ideas. You find career success because you understand human nature and apply this to business. You may not be totally dependable in love, but you do give generously from the heart.

APRIL 10

You're expressive—a thinker, talker, and collector of facts and people. You stir up excitement and aren't afraid of daring action. In love, you're bold and sexy, though secretly you long to be comforted and coddled.

APRIL 11

You have great sparkle and a wonderful way of bringing people together. Curiously, you're the one who takes a long time to trust. Your inner circle knows how sensitive you are. The outer circle sees your charisma.

APRIL 12

You're an entertainer and confidant, and you know how to direct groups. You also possess an elegant romantic spirit, though at least one relationship choice is bound to cause inner suffering. Still, you're promised joy in love.

APRIL 13

You know how to blend, coax, charm, and maneuver. You have great adaptability. You're a reformer who can change the world. Your most troublesome area is that of sexual relationships; here you need to learn how to put head and heart together.

APRIL 14

You're thought of as a character, someone unusual and mesmerizing. Others try to copy your style. In work you're an achiever, and in love you have staying power. You have an "off the wall" reputation but in reality are strong and stable.

APRIL 15

You're a fixer. When you see a need, a problem, a puzzle, you move right in. You're stronger than others, which puts you in the role of a leader. Guard against trying to "remake" your lover. You have control issues to master.

APRIL 16

You're innovative and eccentric, and come alive when in charge of your own thing. You're a detective—you figure out the small details that make a big plan work. In love, you're passionate and deeply romantic, but not steady.

APRIL 17

You have high intellect and deep insight, which gives extra vibrancy to your communication skills. You're demanding of yourself and tend to gravitate toward unusual work. In romantic relationships, you're the dominant one.

APRIL 18

You're serious in your commitments yet lighthearted in your demeanor. You project joy. Beneath this lies a heart that understands struggle and sadness. What makes you heroic is the fact that, despite this, you're not afraid to love.

APRIL 19

You have stamina—you're a real long-distance runner when it comes to work, taking care of others, keeping promises, and pushing toward a goal. You demonstrate your love not in words but in deeds.

YOU AND CHINESE ASTROLOGY

With Marco Polo's adventurous travels in A.D. 1275, Europeans learned for the first time of the great beauty, wealth, history, and romance of China. Untouched as they were by outside influences, the Chinese developed their astrology along different lines from other ancient cultures, such as the Egyptians, Babylonians, and Greeks in whose traditions Western astrology has its roots. Therefore the Chinese zodiac differs from the zodiac of the West. To begin with, it's based on a lunar cycle rather than Western astrology's solar cycle. The Chinese zodiac is divided into twelve years, and each year is represented by a different animal—the rat, ox, tiger, rabbit, dragon, snake, horse, goat, monkey, rooster, dog, or pig. The legend of the twelve animals is that when Buddha lay on his deathbed, he asked the animals of the forest to come and bid him farewell. These twelve were the first to arrive. The cat, as the story goes, is not among the animals because it was napping and couldn't be bothered to make the journey. (In some Asian countries, however, such as Vietnam, the cat replaces the rabbit.)

Like Western astrology, in which the zodiac signs have different characteristics, each of the twelve Chinese animal years assigns character traits specific to a person born in that year. For example, the Year of the Rat confers honesty and an analytical mind, whereas the Year of the Monkey grants charm and a quick ability to spot opportunity.

Here are brief descriptions for Aries for each Chinese animal year:

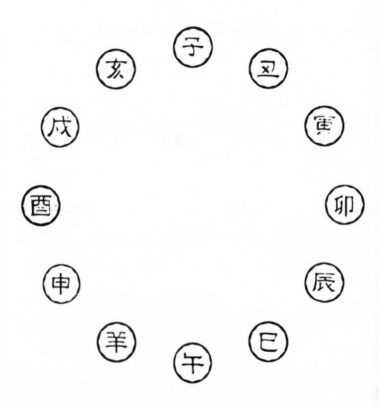

Years of the Rat

1900	1960	2020	
1912	1972	2032	2080
1924	1984	2044	2092
1936	1996	2056	
1948	2008	2068	

Asian lore teaches that the Year of the Rat bestows abundant charm and instant ability to step up to opportunity. This quickness of spirit combines with your Aries assertiveness to make you especially inventive and ambitious. As an Aries Rat, you're full of new ideas and the fire to put them into action. The Year of the Rat is lucky for new beginnings (a time, for example, to get married or launch a new business). Thus, your dynamic Aries propensity for creating change is doubly accented. You strike up instant friendships; you have great warmth and enthusiasm and can easily lead others. In romance, you're impetuously ardent. You believe in love at first sight and will rush toward the one you desire, ignoring the "rules." Compatible partners are born in the Years of the Monkey, Pig, Rat, and Snake.

IF YOU ARE ARIES BORN IN THE YEAR OF THE OX Ⓢ

Years of the Ox

1901	1961	2021	
1913	1973	2033	2081
1925	1985	2045	2093
1937	1997	2057	
1949	2009	2069	

As an Aries, you're fiery and restless, yet being born in the Year of the Ox tempers this with levelheadedness and a drive to find stability. In Asian culture, Ox people are superintelligent, eloquent, and elegant. This, combined with your Aries pioneering spirit, creates someone who inspires others and brings incandescent energy to whatever interests you. You won't even entertain failure—you're single-minded. You're more stubborn than other Ariens, but this also makes you tenacious. Indeed, you are fiercely loyal, and especially in love you are forceful and faithful. Your most outstanding trait is emotionality kept under the rein of a practical approach. Your feelings run deep, and you express them in caring deeds. Compatible partners are born in the Years of the Rabbit, Rooster, Monkey, Pig, and Snake.

IF YOU ARE ARIES BORN IN THE YEAR OF THE TIGER

Years of the Tiger

1902	1962	2022	
1914	1974	2034	2082
1926	1986	2046	2094
1938	1998	2058	
1950	2010	2070	

The Chinese revere the Tiger as the embodiment of courage, abundance, and magnificence. Pregnancies are planned in order to give birth in the Year of the Tiger, which confers charisma and a larger-than-life personality. Many Aries characteristics *are* Tiger qualities, so as an Aries Tiger you are doubly blessed with a spirit of aliveness. You're exciting, intelligent, very persuasive, and highly motivated. You particularly excel in positions where you can create your own kingdom yet be a public figure—for example, in show business or the creative arts. You're an impassioned lover who can also be undisciplined and uncompromising. As a result, your Aries Tiger love life tends to be filled with emotional drama. Compatible partners are born in the Years of the Rabbit, Dog, Dragon, Monkey, Pig, and Tiger.

IF YOU ARE ARIES BORN IN THE YEAR OF THE RABBIT ㊤

Years of the Rabbit

1903	1963	2023	
1915	1975	2035	2083
1927	1987	2047	2095
1939	1999	2059	
1951	2011	2071	

Rabbit people have flash and gregariousness. This doesn't jibe with the Western perception of the rabbit, which is that of a timorous beastie. In Asia, however, the Rabbit personifies cleverness, sociability, a great deal of talent, and an ambitious nature. Your Aries qualities of courage and risk-taking mix wonderfully with Rabbit willingness for following untried paths. As an Aries Rabbit, you're particularly creative—theatrical, gifted at language, and endowed with rich imagination. What sets you apart is your self-control. When you see advantage, you focus on that and won't be diverted. Other Ariens may be distractible, but not you. Love is where you shine, for here you are effusive, sparkling, and romantic. You're abundantly affectionate and want to keep the magic going. Compatible partners are born in the Years of the Goat, Dog, Dragon, Snake, Horse, and Monkey.

IF YOU ARE ARIES BORN IN THE YEAR OF THE DRAGON

Years of the Dragon

1904	1964	2024	
1916	1976	2036	2084
1928	1988	2048	2096
1940	2000	2060	
1952	2012	2072	

Aries and the Dragon are a superstar combination. In Asia, the Dragon is special, for it symbolizes success, high honor, realization of one's dreams, and charismatic allure. As an Aries, you're already born with courage and strong drive to conquer the challenge in front of you—and as an Aries Dragon, you possess extra dynamism, especially when you're dealing with groups of people. You're blessed with self-belief (which is not the same as being egotistical). You have the energy to initiate new projects and are willing to take a chance on your own talents. Aspiration characterizes you. You're also an old-fashioned romantic who believes in true love. In a different era, you'd be called a hero or heroine willing to stake your honor on a person or cause you cherished. Compatible partners are born in the Years of the Rabbit, Goat, Monkey, Snake, and Tiger.

IF YOU ARE ARIES BORN IN THE YEAR OF THE SNAKE

Years of the Snake

1905	1965	2025	
1917	1977	2037	2085
1929	1989	2049	2097
1941	2001	2061	
1953	2013	2073	

In Asia, the Snake is royal—being born in the Year of the Snake confers nobility. Snake people are said to be cultivated, intelligent, and decisive, and to have high goals. You're made of sterner stuff. Combined with your Aries expressiveness and electric vitality, you instantly command attention. Your intuitive mind is your great tool—you instantly analyze and strategize. You do more listening than spouting off, which makes you formidable in the business world and dangerous to competitors. But you have no meanness and, with your humor and fluency of speech, you make friends easily. In love, you are a sentimentalist who adores with your whole being. You want to be safe, however, and you wait to be sure of a lover's loyalty before committing your heart. Compatible partners are born in the Years of the Rabbit, Rooster, Dragon, Horse, Ox, and Rat.

IF YOU ARE ARIES BORN IN THE YEAR OF THE HORSE

Years of the Horse

1906	1966	2026	
1918	1978	2038	2086
1930	1990	2050	2098
1942	2002	2062	
1954	2014	2074	

The Year of the Horse carries extraordinary power. The Chinese believe only those with unusual destinies are born in the Year of the Horse. The Horse symbolizes accomplishment, the gain of respect, and rebellion against the status quo. This, combined with your Aries ability to zoom through hurdles, creates a personality that always stands out. Sometimes you're described as a loose cannon because your drive is to achieve independence. You're brilliant at what you do, generally in an innovative profession in which you're a trendsetter. You're also witty, magnetic, and totally likeable. People follow your lead anywhere. In romantic life, you're impulsive to a fault. Whatever the cost, you pursue your passions (and your lust). Others may gossip, but they secretly admire your courage. Compatible partners are born in the Years of the Rabbit, Rooster, Goat, Horse, and Snake.

IF YOU ARE ARIES BORN IN THE YEAR OF THE GOAT ♈

Years of the Goat

1907	1967	2027	
1919	1979	2039	2087
1931	1991	2051	2099
1943	2003	2063	
1955	2015	2075	

In Asia, the Goat is the charmer, muse, and philosopher, given to invention and a poetic turn of mind. Being born in the Year of the Goat confers an artistic bent and a magical, mystical aura that draws people to you. This integrates seamlessly with your fertile Aries intelligence and sense of adventure. You want to discover and explore and not be practical. Yet curiously, you're very down-to-earth in the way you think, for you strive to make sense of the world and to make your life important. You also appreciate security. You have huge stick-to-it-iveness, but your Aries refusal to be hamstrung by others' rules gives you the reputation of a "mad artist." You're at your best when you can call the shots. In love, you're deeply passionate and committed, though usually you must survive at least one unhappy romantic affair. Compatible partners are born in the Years of the Rabbit, Dragon, Horse, Monkey, and Pig.

IF YOU ARE ARIES BORN IN THE YEAR OF THE MONKEY

申

Years of the Monkey

1908	1968	2028	
1920	1980	2040	2088
1932	1992	2052	2100
1944	2004	2064	
1956	2016	2076	

To be a Monkey person means you're gifted with vivacious charm and a talent for entertaining. The Chinese regard the Monkey as the Messenger—a loquacious, witty, mesmerizing companion who is long on imagination and short on patience for those not as sharp as you. This spellbinding sociability added to your Aries spontaneity and the force with which you initiate makes you a mover and shaker. The Aries Monkey lives in the world of ideas and information. You're a fact finder, but on a deeper level you're the one who explains life to the rest of us. You're the puzzle solver who untangles knotty problems. You adore falling in love at first sight, but to keep passion burning you need an intellectual equal. Your flirtatious nature makes long-term commitment hard going. Compatible partners are born in the Years of the Rabbit, Dragon, Ox, Pig, Rat, and Tiger.

IF YOU ARE ARIES BORN IN THE YEAR OF THE ROOSTER

Years of the Rooster

1909	1957	2005	2053
1921	1969	2017	2065
1933	1981	2029	2077
1945	1993	2041	2089

In Asian mythology, the beloved companion of the Sun is the Rooster, an honor bestowed because of its sincerity. Rooster people are said to be scrupulously honest, brilliant, eloquent, and fascinated with ideas. These qualities blend beautifully with your natural Aries leadership ability. People trust you because you don't break promises. You need order and structure in your life and clear-cut goals to work toward, yet interestingly you can be disorganized and untidy in little ways (a messy desk, for example). You see the big picture but not always the details. You have enormous resilience; never doubt how strong you are. Deep within you is a conservatism—an adherence to a code of ethics. In love, you're dedicated and truthful. You give your whole heart, and a betrayal can be devastating. Compatible partners are born in the Years of the Horse, Ox, and Snake.

Years of the Dog

1910	1958	2006	2054
1922	1970	2018	2066
1934	1982	2030	2078
1946	1994	2042	2090

Like their animal counterparts, Dog people are born with a sense of loyalty and duty. You are a giver—you want to help others and be a support. Friends come to you for your wise advice. Your ability to mold and teach is doubly accented because of your Aries charisma and the fact that you're a creator of change. Born also with Aries superintelligence, you enhance your career using your Dog aptitude for research and uncovering advantageous information. You're good with people because you understand motivation. You could be a counselor but might enjoy politics more because of the power. Basically, though, you don't search for power but for love. You're sentimental, deeply attached, and happiest in a close, committed union. What can bring heartache is your possessiveness. Compatible partners are born in the Years of the Rabbit, Dog, Pig, and Tiger.

IF YOU ARE ARIES BORN IN THE YEAR OF THE PIG 🐷

Years of the Pig

1911	1959	2007	2055
1923	1971	2019	2067
1935	1983	2031	2079
1947	1995	2043	2091

In the West, the pig is low on the totem pole of esteem, but in Asia the Pig is prized for its wisdom, chivalry, and enlightenment. Born in the Year of the Pig, you are characterized as strong, understanding, warm, loving, and hardworking. These lovely attributes are heightened by your Aries gallantry and extraordinary creativity. Your mind sees patterns, and thus you have quick aptitude for both artistic pursuits and business concepts. You're not a loner—indeed, you work well in teams that strive toward a common objective. You're also the most caring friend anyone can have. In romantic affairs, you're a "protector," and nothing is more important than a secure relationship. But you have a way of ignoring warning signals of someone's negative traits, and must be careful about your choices in love. Compatible partners are born in the Years of the Rabbit, Dog, Pig, and Tiger.

YOU AND NUMEROLOGY

Numerology is the language of numbers. It is the belief that there is a correlation between numbers and living things, ideas, and concepts. Certainly, numbers surround and infuse our lives (e.g., twenty-four hours in a day, twelve months of the year, etc.). And from ancient times mystics have taught that numbers carry a *vibration*, a deeper meaning that defines how each of us fits into the universe. According to numerology, you are born with a personal number that contains information about who you are and what you need to be happy. This number expresses what numerology calls your life path.

All numbers reduce to one of nine digits, numbers 1 through 9. Your personal number is based on your date of birth. To calculate your number, write your birth date in numerals. As an example, the birth date of April 17, 1979, is written 1-17-1979. Now begin the addition: $1 + 17 + 1 + 9 + 7 + 9 = 47$; 47 reduces to $4 + 7 = 11$; 11 reduces to $1 + 1 = 2$. The personal number for someone born April 17, 1979, is *Two*.

IF YOU ARE AN ARIES ONE

Keywords: Confidence and Creativity

One is the number of leadership and new beginnings. You rush into whatever engages your heart—whether a new plan, a love affair, or finding more pleasure. Actually, being a One doubles your Aries qualities. You want to have it all, love larger-than-life experiences, and hate the lulls. You're courageous and inventive, and people look to you as a leader. You're attracted to unusual pursuits because you like to be one-of-a-kind. You can't bear to be under the thumb of other people's whims and agendas. Careers you do best in are those in which you can take charge and work independently. As for love, you want ecstasy and passion, and the most exciting part of a flirtation is the beginning.

IF YOU ARE AN ARIES TWO

Keywords: Cooperation and Balance

Two is the number of cooperation and creating a strong entity. Being a Two gives your Aries personality magnetism—you attract what you need. Your magic is not only your people skills, but also your ability to breathe life into empty forms (e.g., a concept, an ambitious business idea, a new relationship) and produce something of worth. In work, you have the smarts and originality to create a project *your* way. You're drawn to careers that combine a business sense with an artistic challenge. In love, you look for a partnership with someone you can trust and share confidences with.

IF YOU ARE AN ARIES THREE

Keywords: Expression and Sensitivity

Three symbolizes self-expression. You have a joyful personality, a gift for words, and a talent for visualization. Being a Three magnifies your Aries ability to dream up concepts and then put your force into making them come true. Creativity and innovation are your specialties. You're a quick study and a quick wit—versatile, mentally active, and curious about the new. You crave stimulation, so you're always on the hunt to discover a new subject or travel somewhere exciting. In love, you need someone who excites you intellectually and sensually, and understands your complex personality.

IF YOU ARE AN ARIES FOUR

Keywords: Stability and Process

Four is the number of dedication and loyalty. It represents *foundation*, exactly as a four-sided square does. You are a builder, and the direction you go in is up. Your method is to learn all you can about a subject and become an expert others respect. In your career, you insist on autonomy over your own work, have an instinct for financial gain, and are superior at judging public taste. Because you rely on yourself, you extend this to being responsible for others. Sexually you're an imaginative and generous lover—and you look for someone who will adore you and head toward the same life goals.

IF YOU ARE AN ARIES FIVE

Keywords: Freedom and Discipline

Five is the number of change and freedom. You want to use your expansive mind to create future projects. Being a Five accentuates your Aries visionary talents. With your chameleon intellect (it can go in any direction), you are different from the ordinary. In whatever you undertake, you were born to play a starring role. Success comes to you because you don't become stuck and know how to let go of what doesn't work. In friendships, you're quick to jump in to give advice. In love, you're uninhibited, frank, and experimental. But you also want a grand passion, to be the center of your partner's life.

IF YOU ARE AN ARIES SIX

Keywords: Vision and Acceptance

Six is the number of teaching, healing, and utilizing your talents. You're geared toward changing the world. Love really does rule your universe, but this does not mean you're a pushover. You're competitive, exacting, and demanding. As a Six, you use your sharp Aries intellect to improve any situation you're in. You always rise to a challenge and always express your own voice. Achieving high goals fills you with happiness. In love, you're fervent about being a helpmate and confidante, as well as a lover. You're also a passionate sensualist who gives your all to someone you trust.

IF YOU ARE AN ARIES SEVEN

Keywords: Trust and Openness

Seven is the number of the mystic and the intensely focused specialist. You have an instinct for problem-solving, and in a flash understand how things work (in business, between people, etc.). You're an intellectual, a philosopher, and connoisseur of everything creative. You like to question and investigate. Being a Seven amplifies your Aries ability to communicate ideas and put them to use creating original work. At your core you're extremely loyal and intensely loving. Your deepest need is for a partner who'll stay by your side on your journey to becoming splendid.

IF YOU ARE AN ARIES EIGHT

Keywords: Abundance and Power

Eight is the number of mastery and authority. You are intelligent, alert, quick in action, born to take power in your own hands and guide traffic into the direction you want. As an Eight, you have extra Aries power to think big and tackle the hard stuff. Others sense you're the one who knows best, and they're right. Major decisions don't faze you because you like challenge and aren't afraid of risk. You have a passion for enlargement—which may include adding to your education and enjoying the limelight. You're a very sexual being, hugely responsive, passionate, sensitive to your partner's needs, and a magnificent lover.

IF YOU ARE AN ARIES NINE

Keywords: Integrity and Wisdom

Nine is the path of the "old soul," the number of completion and full bloom. Because it's the last number, it sums up the highs and lows of human experience, and you live a life of dramatic events. You're very intellectual, deeply feeling, extremely protective, interested in all kinds of exploration. People see you as colorful and gallant because you have an adventurous outlook but are also spiritual and altruistic. You'll forgive any weakness in others as long as they are honest with you. In love, you're truthful and sincere—and also a romantic, highly sensual creature.

Aries

LAST WORD: YOUR ARIES UNFINISHED BUSINESS

Psychologists often use the phrase *unfinished business* to describe unresolved issues—for example, patterns from childhood that cause unhappiness, anger that keeps one stuck, or scenarios of family dysfunction that repeat through second and third generations (such as alcoholism or abusive behavior).

Astrology teaches that the past is indeed very much with us in the present—and that using astrological insights can help us move out of emotional darkness into greater clarity. Even within this book (which is not a tome of hundreds of pages) you have read of many of the superlatives and challenges of being Aries. You have breathtaking gifts, and at the same time certain tendencies that can undermine utilizing these abilities.

In nature, a fascinating fact is that in jungles and forests a poisonous plant will grow in a certain spot, and always just a few feet away is a plant that is the antidote to that specific poison. Likewise, in astrology, the antidote is right there, ready to be used when the negatives threaten to overwhelm your life.

Aries's unfinished business has to do with entitlement and arrogance ("I deserve this!"). Aries has a selfish mindlessness—being what classical astrology calls a "primitive daredevil." You want freedom from rules and restraints. You look for the frothy excitement of yet another romantic relationship. You rush impatiently toward a challenge you know nothing about. You thrill to the frisson of leaping into danger (e.g., a forbidden love affair). You can be heedless.

People around you always sense your Aries bent for the thing that stimulates. Actor Russell Crowe, an Aries, in describing how he chooses his roles, recently said, "If I don't get the goose-bump factor when reading the script, then I can't do it."

All human beings are self-oriented (it's our survival instinct), but Aries's energies seem to spring totally from a self point of view. The most frequently used words in your conversation are *I* and *me*. Aries is the sign of *self* and your vision is yourself. This self-involvement is like a speeding train. When your attention is seized by something you want, something that strikes your fancy, you tend to behave like a greedy baby. Your Aries quality of being childlike is charming, but charm wears thin with childish behavior. *Childlike* means spontaneous, open to the new, filled with wonder. *Childish* means bratty, avaricious, ill behaved—unwilling to share and play nicely.

Yet the antidotes are there, to be found in their entirety in being Aries—in your boldness and courage. Webster's dictionary defines courage as the quality of facing danger and difficulties instead of withdrawing from them. You're the one who runs *into* the burning building. You tell the truth instead of sweeping it under the rug. You're the rush of adrenaline that comes with a launch—of an untried project or a travel adventure or a trip to the moon!

That impetus comes from an expansive vision. You're a crusader, an enemy of the small-minded. Your thinking is direct; you don't let gray clouds of hesitation confuse you. You minimize the problems and, like a laser beam, zap toward the goal. You're determined to dominate over what scares you.

Also, your Aries unfinished business is everything you're still on the way to accomplishing. Astrology teaches that you were born to change the world. In small gestures and large acts, your life will change others' lives. You're spontaneous with your kindness and abundantly generous (qualities that coexist with your self-orientation). Your "can do" approach can create business enterprises, artistic innovation, career success, and financial security. Your passionate ability to love nourishes relationships and family life that will become your deepest satisfactions. All this is part of your unfinished business.

FAMOUS PEOPLE WITH THE SUN IN ARIES

Maya Angelou
Johann Sebastian Bach
Alec Baldwin
Warren Beatty
Marlon Brando
Matthew Broderick
Charles Chaplin
Cesar Chavez
Tom Clancy
Billy Collins
Joan Crawford
Russell Crowe
Clarence Darrow
Bette Davis
Doris Day
Daniel Day-Lewis
Isak Dinesen
Celine Dion
David Frost
Robert Frost
James Garner
John Gielgud

Alec Guinness
Hugh Hefner
Billie Holiday
Harry Houdini
Henry James
Thomas Jefferson
Elton John
Keira Knightley
David Letterman
Ali MacGraw
Peyton Manning
Eugene McCarthy
Steve McQueen
Ann Miller
Dudley Moore
Eddie Murphy
Leonard Nimoy
Rosie O'Donnell
Sarah Jessica Parker
Danica Patrick
Gregory Peck
Anthony Perkins

Mary Pickford
Colin Powell
Sergei Rachmaninoff
Diana Ross
Omar Sharif
Stephen Sondheim
Edward Steichen
Rod Steiger
Gloria Steinem
Leopold Stokowski
Gloria Swanson
Arturo Toscanini
Spencer Tracy
Peter Ustinov
Ludwig Mies Van Der Rohe
Vincent van Gogh
Andrew Lloyd Webber
Thornton Wilder
Tennessee Williams
Florenz Ziegfeld

PART TWO

ALL ABOUT YOUR SIGN OF ARIES

ARIES'S ASTROLOGICAL AFFINITIES, LINKS, AND LORE

SYMBOL: The Ram

Assertive, sexual, able to climb to great heights. In Greek mythology, the Golden Fleece is the fleece of the golden-haired, winged ram.

RULING PLANET: Mars ♂

The ancient god of war, aggression, and conflict, Mars signifies virility and vitality. It represents physicality, sex drive, and forcefulness. Our word martial is derived from Mars, as is the month of March; in the early Roman calendar, March was the first month of the year. In astrology, the influence of Mars denotes courage, passion, and competition. It governs boldness and the will to win, as well as the ability to turn ideas into action. It can foster tension and accidents, and rules over fire and danger.

DOMINANT KEYWORD

I AM

GLYPH (WRITTEN SYMBOL): ♈

The pictograph represents the horns and long nose of the Ram. It also pictures the eyebrows and nose of the human face. (The head is the part of anatomy that Aries rules.) This was an ancient pictograph of a human being with outstretched hands, a representation of new life and striving for light. In symbolic terms, the glyph is two half-moons joined by a straight line, which indicates idealism tied to authority and leadership.

PART OF THE BODY RULED BY ARIES: The Head

Aries people are prone to headaches and subject to minor injuries around the head and face. An Aries tends to have healthy, vibrant hair.

LUCKY DAY: Tuesday

The day named for Mars (Tiw, in the Old Norse—thus, Tiw's Day). Mars is the ruler of Aries.

LUCKY NUMBERS: 1 and 9

Numerologically, 1 is the number of new beginnings, and 9 is linked to heroism and passion. These qualities align with the nature of Aries.

TAROT CARD: The Emperor

The card in the Tarot linked to Aries is the Emperor. Ancient names for this card are Son of the Morning and Chief Among the Mighty. In the Tarot this card points to release of energy and taking action. The Emperor is an authority figure that embodies strength, dynamic leadership, and getting the job done. The Emperor's qualities are courage and an indomitable spirit. In a Tarot reading, this card says someone or something will bring influence and action resulting in the realization of the desired goal.

The card itself pictures a regal male figure wearing a crown and sitting on a throne decorated with rams' heads (the ram is the emblem of Mars, ruling planet of Aries). In the Emperor's right hand is a scepter in the shape of an Egyptian ankh (the Cross of Life), and in his left an orb representing dominion.

For Aries, the Emperor tells you to be a responsible leader, that you have deep life force, and that you are the one who can make your intentions and wishes come true.

MAGICAL BIRTHSTONE: Diamond

A precious gemstone treasured for its superlative brilliance, clarity, and hardness—so hard it is used as a measure of the toughness of other stones. The name diamond is derived from an ancient Greek word meaning "unbreakable" and "untamable." The diamond is extremely beautiful, for it disperses white light into all the colors of the spectrum and seems to radiate fire. Diamonds are among the costliest of jewels. For thousands of years diamonds have been worn as symbols of power, given as tokens of love, and used as a talisman to protect against danger, especially damage from lightning and fire. For Aries, this jewel attracts love, financial success, and brings good fortune in new ventures. The diamond is particularly lucky for Aries when worn on the left side of the body.

SPECIAL COLOR: Red

The color of fire and excitement. Red signifies vitality, life force, energy, and passion.

CONSTELLATION OF ARIES

Aries is the Latin word for *ram*, and in Greek mythology is named after the golden, winged ram that rescued the king Phrixos. Courage and daring are part of the Aries character. Ancient Chinese and Babylonians believed that when the world first began, the constellation of Aries was in the center of the heavens. Thus, they taught that Aries was the most powerful sign in the zodiac.

CITIES

Florence, Naples, Verona, Marseilles

COUNTRIES

England, Germany, Poland

FLOWERS

Geranium, Honeysuckle, Sweet Pea

TREES

All thorn-bearing trees

HERBS AND SPICES

Mustard, Cayenne Pepper, Capers

METAL: Iron

Symbolizing life force and strength, from antiquity iron has been linked to the god Mars. The written symbols for iron and for the planet Mars (ruler of Aries) are the same. Iron is one of the primary constituents of blood; the metal and the liquid smell similar, and it has long been called the blood of the earth. From ancient times, iron has been perceived as the life force of the earth itself. It had the reputation of repelling malevolent entities (witches, ghosts, evil spirits). Old myths say the gift of blacksmithing—the art of working with iron through fire—was given to humans by the gods.

ANIMALS RULED BY ARIES

Sheep and, especially, rams

DANGER

Aries people are susceptible to harm from fire and sharp instruments. You're also prone to accidents involving high speed, and have a predilection for getting into violent and dangerous situations.

PERSONAL PROVERB

All glory comes from daring to begin.

KEYWORDS FOR ARIES

Pioneering leader
Highly motivated
Competitive
Forceful
Abundant energy
Keen sense of humor
The power to begin
Needs challenge
Optimistic
Aims for the top
A winner
Courageous
Impatient
Arrogant
Blunt
Hair-trigger temper
Selfish
Easily bored
Impetuous
Creates high level of romance in relationships
Passionate
Volatile sexuality

HOW ASTROLOGY SLICES AND DICES YOUR SIGN OF ARIES

DUALITY: Masculine

The twelve astrological signs are divided into two groups, *masculine* and *feminine*. Six are masculine and six are feminine; this is known as the sign's *duality*. A masculine sign is direct and energetic. A feminine sign is receptive and magnetic. These attributes were given to the signs about 2,500 years ago. Today modern astrologers avoid the sexism implicit in these distinctions. A masculine sign does not mean "positive and forceful" any more than a feminine sign means "negative and weak." In modern terminology, the masculine signs, such as your sign of Aries, are defined as outer-directed and strong through action. The feminine signs are self-contained and strong through inner reserves.

TRIPLICITY (ELEMENT): Fire

The twelve signs are also divided into groups of three signs. Each of these three-sign groups is called a *triplicity*, and each of these denotes an *element*. The elements are *Fire*, *Earth*, *Air*, and *Water*. In astrology, an element symbolizes a fundamental characterization of the sign.

The three *Fire* signs are Aries, Leo, and Sagittarius. Fire signs are active and enthusiastic.

The three *Earth* signs are Taurus, Virgo, and Capricorn. Earth signs are practical and stable.

The three *Air* signs are Gemini, Libra, and Aquarius. Air signs are intellectual and communicative.

The three *Water* signs are Cancer, Scorpio, and Pisces. Water signs are emotional and intuitive.

QUADRUPLICITY (QUALITY): Cardinal

The twelve signs are also divided into groups of four signs. Each of these four-sign groups is called a *quadruplicity*, and each of these denotes a *quality*. The qualities are *Cardinal*, *Fixed*, and *Mutable*. In astrology, the quality signifies the sign's interaction with the outside world.

Four signs are *Cardinal** signs. These are Aries, Cancer, Libra, and Capricorn. Cardinal signs are enterprising and outgoing. They are the initiators and leaders.

---

*When the Sun crosses the four cardinal points in the zodiac, we mark the beginning of each of our four seasons. Your sign of Aries begins spring; Cancer begins summer; Libra begins fall; Capricorn begins winter.

Four signs are *Fixed*. These are Taurus, Leo, Scorpio, and Aquarius. Fixed signs are resistant to change. They hold on; they're perfectors and finishers, rather than originators.

Four signs are *Mutable*. These are Gemini, Virgo, Sagittarius, and Pisces. Mutable signs are flexible, versatile, and adaptable. They are able to adjust to differing circumstances.

Your sign of Aries is a Masculine, Fire, Cardinal sign—and no other sign in the zodiac is this exact combination. Your sign is a one-of-a-kind combination, and therefore you express the characteristics of your duality, element, and quality differently from any other sign.

For example, your sign is a *Masculine* sign, meaning you are active and assertive. You're a *Fire* sign, meaning you're excitable, energetic, and passionate. And you're a *Cardinal* sign, meaning you're outgoing and open to new experiences.

Now the sign of Leo is also Masculine and Fire, but unlike Aries (which is Cardinal), Leo is Fixed. Therefore, like you, Leo is extroverted and passionate—and radiates a fiery excitement—but Leo is also more stubborn in its opinions, convinced of being on the side of truth. Leo's need is to "self-create," which means its ego is invested in its objectives. The goals become who Leo *is*, and therefore this sign becomes fixated on its ambitions. With its intense focus, Leo is certainly not as willing as you are to abandon an unworkable plan and go on to something new. You, being Cardinal, are energized by innovation and new beginnings. There's nothing you like better than getting rid of what slows you down and taking off in an unexplored direction. Your sign of Aries represents propelling forward, and your motivation is to instigate and inspire.

Sagittarius, too, is Masculine and Fire, but unlike Aries (which is Cardinal), Sagittarius is Mutable. Like you, Sagittarius loves exploring new ideas and approaches life with enthusiasm. Both signs jump in first and think later, and both look for freedom of expression. But being Mutable, Sagittarius is changeable and inconsistent, and can scatter its energy. Sagittarius's interests fly out in many directions, and it can easily be sidetracked from its immediate goals. Thus, it often has trouble being responsible and is known for leaving unfinished projects in its wake. You are a Cardinal sign, famous for being a go-getter. You have a way of minimizing problems and heading straight toward the center of a project. You take action. You have a positive attitude and, unless you decide the end result isn't worth the effort, the power to make what you envision happen.

POLARITY: Libra

The twelve signs are also divided into groups of two signs. Each of these two-sign groups is called a *polarity* (meaning "opposite"). Each sign in the zodiac has a polarity, which is its opposite sign in the other half of the zodiac. The two signs express opposite characteristics.

Aries and Libra are a polarity. Aries is the sign of self. You are positive and dynamic and operate from a self-centered perspective. That is, you approach life according to what *you* believe is true and possible. You strongly project your own personality. Old textbooks say that Aries's flight is toward glory—you are here to produce outstanding work and be a shining example. Astrologically, Aries is likened to a newborn bursting with life.

Being ardent and passionate, you're drawn to relationships. But a great part of this impulse is to be admired and encouraged in your high deeds. In romance, you also love the chase and can rather quickly grow weary of an affair. In essence, Aries is a "me first" sign, and you find it difficult to blend yourself into another or give up any of your "self." You are full of feelings but can be blind to what another is feeling.

Libra, your opposite sign, is the sign of partnerships and re-lationships. Libra is outer-directed—its energies are focused on melding and combining with people. This is the sign that seeks sharing and cooperation; it rules alliances, associations, agree-ments, and the pooling of resources. Librans feel incomplete without an *other*—a partner, lover, mate, intimate companion. They are empowered by being part of a union. Libra is charming and easygoing, diplomatic, and sensitive to others. Born under the sign of equilibrium, Librans are the peacemakers and mediators and strive to maintain harmony.

Astrologically, you as an Aries can benefit from adopting some of Libra's grace with people. Libra instinctively has a way of mak-ing others feel important and cared about; Libra knows how to listen and give compliments. It understands the other's need to be recognized. Aries is often perceived as pushy, and you run into situations where people are turned off and back away from you. By learning from Libra's example of inviting the other in (rather than ramming what you want at them), you'll receive far more cooperation. People will soften toward you, want to be included in your plans, become followers and fans.

Often your self-aggrandizement takes up so much space there isn't room for anyone else. Yet you do need approval and apprecia-tion, and you want to be cared about. You have a great and gener-ous heart and are thrilled to help others out. This is the side of your personality you can develop to its full potential with the help of Libra's enchanting predilection for pleasing others.

In turn, Libra has much to learn from you. High on this list are your Aries confidence, your ability to push through obstacles, and your courage to speak your mind. Libra is so intent on being liked, it allows others to take over. Libra will say yes just to keep the peace. Being conciliatory, Libra backs away from conflict with a smiling face but inwardly feeling put upon, misunderstood, and invisible. It gives its power away and then is secretly resentful. You, Aries, are willing to take a stance, to be direct and truthful and charge right in. Being liked is fine, but being the winner is all. You are a brash force of nature!